Out of the Fog

POEMS OF NATURE, NURTURE AND IMAGINATION

JILL UCHIYAMA

TRANSFORMATIONS PRESS

ISBN: 9798362957469

Published in Wenham, Massachusetts by Transformations Press.
Email: info@transformationspress.org
Web: transformationspress.org

Printed in the United States of America

The term 'being in the fog' is often used to describe the way adoptees feel, think, operate and relate before they come out of the denial, conditioning and ignorance that cloaks the impacts of adoption.

For Sean and Janice

Contents

From the Window Above

Not Yours

I am not yours
though I swim and suck a sludge
thumb inside of you.
Your thoughts unchewed,
suckled through the straw of your belly.
But I am not your words, cannot see
from the rocky eyes in this fitted brain,
tight as fish buds.
I am your inner puppy, blind
as we walk through the streets of Manhattan.
Here I rent your time,
inch down the canal like a stripper pole
ready for action,
remembering in body,
not in mind.
I am only yours
until they pull me away from your love cast.
A deaf promise,
a dumb lotus,
so alive.

Relinquishment

Stranger that birthed me
damp with saline and amniotic fluid,
might have held me tightly as a football
may have taken one long look
into the honey coating of my eyes
too small to receive her,
and photographically
memorized me, bottom to head.
On that day, I am taken from soreness
which will grow into more soreness,
nightgown falling loosely from my home.
We become like grain and glass
washed away from the conch,
root and pulp
pulled apart from the skin,
stretched
as far as we can possibly stretch.

Baby Lady

A social worker flew me
from New York City to Indiana,
my parents not knowing her proper name,
simply called her *The Baby Lady*.
I imagine the new nervous parents peeking
into bassinets of baby eyes, hands, tufts of hair,
miniature grandparents gone backward in time.
We are the soft parcels waiting to be moved.
Parentless air babies
kept alive by shift workers.
The chosen lady, maybe
the most experienced Baby Lady
packed a little bag inside her own valise
with first baby things donated by nice people:
talc for buffing skin, little comb to sweep the hair.
Maybe someone noticed me in her arms
and congratulated her as if we had made it
through the screaming journey together.
Maybe I cried all the way to Indiana,
strapped into her warm lap, my Filomena
riding the bounce of jet stream together
erasing New York in the shearing flow.
Maybe she held me tighter to cushion the fall
from one place to another,
the way Life holds up life between stories.

Big Brown Chair

The first time I felt compassion
Winnie the Pooh was on TV,
voice slowed by honey,
no friends to come to his party.
I remember this first sound of heartbreak,
a cartoon bear's lament
sawing through my little girl solar plexus,
small as a cricket's cage.
At four or five, hardly aware of the world of otherness,
the universe too far away
though it had made me,
I knelt behind that big brown chair
hiding the weeping from my mother.
Hugging its bulk as it enveloped me,
I pressed my sadness into its burly back,
holding the dead skin of my family,
hair from our dog and cat.
As the emotional transfer took place
the chair sat strong and dumb
soiled and emptied upon in the TV light.
I was lighter for it, the chair—
the father who never learned to comfort.

Not Mine

You are not mine,
though I dream of you
dear Mother, unicorn of unreality-
You appear on a bus
or a butter aisle,
you're the lady at the bank.
You enter my dreams uninvited, slipping
me off my leash until the morning.
You are not mine
as my mother toasts the pop tarts,
holding you in the back of my throat,
a small animal I cannot let be seen.
You're there, stamped
in the passport of my face-
my latitude,
water colored into each pen of wavy hair.
You dissolve like Christ on the thick of my tongue,
in the long-ness of night, where I fish tail back to your waters.
You are still there in a smile
or a dot on my small, flecked arm,
on my breath, in my breath
though I swear I'd never find you.

Incarnation Vow

If we choose our parents
from before birth
then I imagine you both
the night you conceived me.
Loose clothes around the car-
my chosen womb and handsome seed.
From the window above
I could have willed this,
could have whispered
through the crack of light between your legs:

Dear borrowed bodies
She is not your wife.
He is not your husband.
Though we'll never be together again after this first night,
I'll place you in the Cosmos where I can always find you—
Swimming like two secret spoons I needed.

Real Mother

Was she really adopted?
My young friend asks
The train of private feelings   hidden
slams into a parked throat.

Mother looks down on the child,
then the mountain looks away.
i am nine, my stomach,
a roller coaster car dangling   before the fall.

Here is an edge
which i cannot go back to,
a story you can never unknow.
Pulling out the fresh bulbs, she plants
her feelings deeply in the soil next to mine:

Do not tell people you are adopted,
It makes me feel as though I'm not your real mother.

i listen and follow our dog   out of the room.

Up to my pink bedroom a needle spins on a record,
practice my name again and again
in different handwriting.

Loyalty

For most of her life my mother
set her hair in electric blue curlers
dried in the standard hair dryer,
teased out to Mexico.
Her reddish- brown fuzz
piled like a bee's hive,
deflated ever so slightly through the years.
My brother and I joked about it,
getting lost from her was impossible.
The hair rose above store aisles
bouncing like cotton candy,
too serious to eat.
Sprayed stiff to stay together,
mom appeared with us near the clouds.
The hair held up through Christmas's and birthdays-
proudly perfect at my wedding
softened through my divorce,
absorbing my pain like a mop.
For years I left mom behind at bus stops,
tears of grief erupting from her Irish face,
burning and collapsing in the parting.
One time she left me,
standing at the depot
I watched her hair grow
smaller and smaller as the bus drove away.

Blue Eyes, Brown Eyes

She cried at commercials.
Cried when feral Pearly
mewed to death under the deck.
Eyes spilling over with water,
loose like a backyard spigot.
Her eyes were as deep blue
as the Hawaiian nights of her twenties
black in the middle, reaching
into waves, dolphins diving.
Mine emerged from an olive face,
piles of earth soaking in the oils
of everyone's emotions.
Politely, we pretended not to see our differences.
Avoided laying eyes on our bare breasts.
We are a cat and her bunny child
like Koko and her kitten, we're the way
all mothers and their strange children
come to the table, hungry
before the world gets fed.

Quickie

We made it to Queens in Bruce's red Escort
landed at the seedy motel.
In the room we had a quickie
and then a baked potato from a local shop.
At a cheap honeymoon diner in the morning,
cigarettes and coffee, I picked up
the arm of a payphone, honking
an impossible f in my ear.
There, I searched for two strangers
in a city of eight million
as the phone book dented my arm.
We were nineteen, and already
worn down by the size of this project.
Giving up, we slipped
to the back of the Statue in New Jersey.
Feeling the city in my bones
I quickly gave her the finger
and then I gave one to the city,
to anyone who refused to show her face.

The Bronx

Every year our Indiana teachers asked
our name, birthday, birthplace-
The replies sat in my mouth
like hardened gum waiting to be stretched
projected, across the desk,
direct to my teacher's ear.
I never said *The Bronx* but *New York City*,
fearful of scaring my classmates.
As soon as I let out my secret
the class stirred like rocks in a noisy cocktail
a snicker, and ghostly staring.
Some child scoffed as if I were a liar,
and I ducked
from the dodge ball
of doubt and disbelief.
Years later when we sat in Bruce's car
where Fordham hospital used to be,
I faced it, a voice from within:
This was my birthplace, damn you.

Happy Camper

My father tugged his fishing boat
behind a bitchy truck, to dunk
his rod in the quiet cool lakes of Minnesota.
When he'd come back, buckets
of silvery trophies, fresh perch
sloshed and spilt on the kitchen floor.
To capacity, he'd fill the sink-
drop in the dead, the almost dead
and the assaulted with a soft watery thud.
Degraded fins torn, eyes rolled back
compadres floating sideways, except one guy
bobbing among his dead friends.
An atheist, my father recoiled
from the way some said God made the world.
Rolled his eyes at how Jesus fed all those people,
scoffed as water turned to wine.
On Saturdays, he hunted mushrooms
early in the quiet wood. I doubt he heard
the clammy stems scream
from the plucking of their roots.
Doubt he heard the hooks gently pierce the
soft crook of their mouths.
Doubt he'd heard my reply on the phone
soon after he asked,
Are you a happy camper?

Watching My Father Die

When I saw my father on his deathbed
arms limp,
legs in a triangle
broken like a horse-
I recalled when my hamster passed away.
Watching his still white body for a sign,
my finger stroked the shock of death.
But here in my father's room,
the Indiana cornfields
were golden in the sun,
and the oxygen cup danced over his mouth
which used to yell and kiss me.
Around his ears was a little blue elastic
keeping it all together.
We sat, the three of us talking like normal
conscious
of all the time in the world,
all the air on the planet
while he deflated moment by moment,
a soft balloon slipping away from its mouthpiece.
He fell so deliberately flat
now that we were there.
It was amazing.
It was simple.
We came. He went.

Within the hour we were not four,
but three.
The nurse removed the elastic
to let in the transition,
the struggle falling closer to its end.
I could not take my eyes off
his newly dead face,
forehead still hot with activity.
I expected something colder, faster,
more decidedly gone,
a sign of where he
hovered around us.
But there was nothing to see
except my kiss
blown away by his last exhale.

The Good Stuff

The DNA kit was like a box full of birthdays.
First the little vial, squeaking out of its home,
then the solution in plastic waiting to be released.
Outside my window the birds settled down.
Gently, I pulled my hair back,
opened my mouth
to spit into the little tubular opening,
all the questions of my life.
I spit again, coming up for air and more saliva,
the good stuff collecting into happy bubbles
shining and bright.
I spat until I filled the line, until
we were both satisfied with the amount,
examined the DNA as it began to tell stories to itself
tiny helixes tossed but in-tact.
Capping the sample with a snap,
I kissed it goodbye in its little box,
the Cosmos already wise to its secrets.
In California, a lab worker throws the brave
ancestral liquid into a silicon spinner,
shards of shared human stories
dance and bounce apart in the breaking.
I imagine in that soup, deep in time
Neanderthals shaping their tools of flint
banging out progress and new dreams.

Reindeer herders talking to the sky.
There our human story spins out rays
the way the merry-go-round at school took
your running legs wildly off the ground.
There in that galaxy which hugs us to life
each human, every being wonders
wonders about their mother.

The Packet

There is a packet yellow and puffy
stuffed in my mailbox in the August heat.
I pulled it out and toward me-
the father I have never known.
You entered my living room
falling out of the stack of pages
a mug shot introduction
like an Ace of Spades.
For the first time we looked at each other through celluloid.
Your eyes half closed,
big and brown,
full lips and Adam's apple jutting out,
half of a handshake from the soft
curve of your neck, one curl
cut short and smashed by Bristol Cream.
As the long search ends something in me opens
through the grave which stations you.
Time turns back and forward
as your face became mine.
I had seen you in the mirror
every morning,
in my eyes squinting in the sun.
And now, I can undress you
little packet

in place of a father
and pour some more wine.
You rest in my hands
and in the notes which play this piano.
I found my answers
through your neat cursive writing-
Next to number of children, you wrote:
None

I Loved My Brother

I loved my brother when I went to his room,
listening to the records,
the grooves moving past another year.
Around the sun, around
our parkway, chinking out stories-
My brother made me forget the behind, the before.
We blended invisibly, his wet face waiting
for me to jump in the water, already ahead
in years, in miles, in breath.
Down the icy path he'd carved on a disc,
my blazing brother came direct
from my mother's womb.
I did not.
His likeness passed into his children
while mine stayed frozen in my childless form.
But who cares.
I loved my brother for loving his children.
For writing in my life this new script.
For his serious moustache and chest pumped by iron,
a piece of furniture, strong
made from all things one can count on.
The day he lost his first born
just hours after her arrival,
I remembered this:
He was the first boy that held me.

First Talk

I was watching Oprah when you called.
An unknown California number which
I casually answered, as if I had not been waiting
all my life for you.
This was the beginning of my middle age,
nearly 50 and you are 67, younger
than my own mother,
who could stand over you like another mother.
You said hello, and then my name and within an instant
you and I were reunited.
Your sweet voice welcomed me
like a hotel resort that you want to stay in forever.
Breathlessly, I moved to the kitchen stool.
Listened to you joyfully chatter
as the hot blood collected in my ears.
You were already talking my heart down,
easing the shock from the wild arcing wires.
We spoke excitedly like two girls
brushing out the sounds of our lost conversation,
squeezing laughs out of our throats
first small, then growing fondly free.
The corners of our mouths pulling loose from the weeds
from silent, buried eddies of lost years and stories.
Finally, above the laws
we unleash like two fresh creeks

ready to spill into new land.
You were here, now,
cupped in my hands
on a phone on an ordinary day.
Me on one coast, you on the other,
breathing in my ear.

Most This Amazing Day

I see you on the other side of the encased glass.
Your absurd teenage body coveting the coming
of my newly born baby body,
slick and slipping like confetti through your hands.
We were once two similar keys,
plunged into a drop box of destiny.
Neither one of us choosing, or feeling
or choosing to feel,
pushed away from the dock,
you in one direction, I in the other.
Today I pass over each united state
waiting to break the brittle bones of our contract.
I will touch down in the West and there you will be,
inviting me into your car.
Our hearts, two wild horses run free.
For all the poets I have loved,
for the days of DNA unmatched
for this damn life hiding from plain sight-
we are at last
two women, two puzzle pieces
trunks and waists reunited,
arms deft and reaching
calling into the canyon of one lost past.

Tabula Rasa

Blank Walls

Leave them bare
    life will create your story,
decorate you.

The Universe waits to know you
without complaint

This is my lineage-
   silence talking to the future

Friendship

This is friendship
two people
laughing at walls

Riding the changes,
looking past the flaws.

Holding intimacy

between meetings.

Adoption

This is adoption-
me on the wall
interspersed with strangers

Marketing myself
to be loved

grateful
for a colonized life.

Reunification

This is reunification-
me on your cell phone,
not on your wall.

Looking in the mirror,
ancestors emerge.

Hearing mother's voice again.

Relinquishment

This is relinquishment-
smelling every human
in search of my mother.

Colon

tied in

knots-

Hypersensitivity.

Self-Knowledge

This is self-knowledge-

hearing another's story,

deeply.

Grief

Two people who cannot keep a child.

Two people who cannot make a child.

Two people who cannot change a child.

Brutality

This is brutality-
no one remembers you
those first 45 days.

Waiting to find them.

Waiting to meet them.

Waiting to know them.

Abandoned.

(again and again)

Courage

letting everything be
in order to feel.

This is courage-
Coming out of the fog.

Out of the Fog

Window Box

My father built boxes
with stained wood and black hinges.
Mine was a window box,
painted thickly with white strokes,
creaking open in hot weather, swollen sides.
Mine contained music records and ethnic dolls
with faces that were trying to look like us.
Mom-made pillows for the top of it,
circles, squares, and hearts
as if there were not enough ways to love me-
I am an adopted girl, shaped and tailored
by nature and nurture and imagination.
My father built a box of love around me,
to contain me, as he'd sit at Old Glory most nights.
Once my mother got a handmade box,
a small redwood box, emptied of jewels and music-
inside, a forgiveness letter I read through the years.
My brother got a whole room-box, and one for the car.
There was even a box for Pearly,
and one for Alex too,
little cat coffins shielded from the wind,
from the cold,
the cold ground.

The Bracelet (for Sean)

Today I point my car in your old direction
two hours on highways until I reach Starbucks
and Pencey's where I showed you the taco spices.
You would be wounded to know that McLaddens is gone-
since all roads led to craft beer.

But that was five years ago and now I am here alone
without you, and not just alone because you are not here-
alone because you are no more.

For 20 years as you led the nursery
you walked, through these posh shops.
You got tea and I got boba.
Today in that kitchen store where I once bought the scissors,
a cross woman scorns me under her mask.

You might have been there with me
standing in the corner, hands in pockets saying,
"See?" And maybe I would understand a bit better.
Maybe this is a town with rich angry people,
afraid of other people. Terrified of germs.

Maybe it is the people who pushed you to go West,
or why you adored the weirdness of Portland.

As I walk, I look for the paper, for the death notice
which I wrote myself, one year after you took your life.

I walk and walk, opening plastic news bins, empty and dry.
And in the library, I find only old papers on the shelves,
as if life stood still once you were gone.

I need fresh. I need yesterday.
I need you to walk me over to the Indian place for one final meal.

Instead, I bought a blue bracelet like one of yours
with Celtic knots for beads and cosmic globes.

Reminds me of how we met,
something comes again from nothing.

Wrong Heaven

I'm sliding the photos out of tight sleeves
they crinkle and stick in protest
one by one, I slip them out.
How efficiently they line up in order,
the children we never had.
Japan 1999
Okasan, Otosan, me and you.
Those years shorter than miles
fewer than pictures-
You pouring tea on New Years, as I pick at
the great Osechi, a banquet of fish and eggs
meant for making us fertile.
Then, I never admitted
the backward magnets of our cultures.
How fast it would all be over.
How soon I said those impossible words
spilling out like teeth I tried hard to keep.
You behind the screen door, I entered the car.
Pictures in a scanner, finally placed in a cloud,
marching toward their wrong idea of heaven.

The Sale

My brother is glad to be rid of it,
moldy basement, little shit squirrels breaking in
to steal our sanity, this house
where my parents practiced
dancing for my wedding
on the round braided rug.
This is where my father wallpapered year after year
on scaffolding like a tightrope walker.
This is where our dog peed
uncontrollably on Christmas
the day before we put him down.
This house is not for sale.
These memories are not for everyone.
They linger like the scent of my father's tobacco,
mother's lilac lotion smacked on her thighs.
This house contained our youth.
Where the fireplace crackled while we ate fried chicken
and I learned to listen to grandpa repeat stories.
This was where we schooled ourselves,
where my father cooked fish and mom cleaned up.
This was the house for the cats when I could not keep them.
There is no price for this house.
There is no bargain here, no sale,
no grave in which to place this home.
This was the only home I've known.

Despite my love for it.
Despite the years I cleaned
and cared about it.
This was where we lived
to grow into different people.
Where two blue birds sat
on that mini gravestone in the backyard,
next to my father's benches
hopping into another world.

Breathing

We are invisibly together today
as the wind whips quietly outside the wings,
formless and floating at 32,000 feet.
When I last saw your hair
it was damp from gasping,
now air is all around.
The lights down below
dot the Illinois landscape, sanded
down and stretched out like a motherboard.
I can feel the electricity coursing
through each family's home.
It is Thanksgiving
and the first without you, Dad.
I bend my face down to your collar
to smell your body still lingering
on your old gray sweatshirt, now mine.
For a moment, we are perfectly balanced
between the physical, non-physical.
Between Air and the suffocation.

Ode to the Colon
(after Sharon Olds)

I did not want to write to you
Oh, colon, oh dark one,
but there you were, coiled like a shy old cat
ready to spring into action.
You were always in the background, thankless.
Not like the heart, or the Soul
which had countless lyrics after them,
lifetimes of poets swooning over their content and shape, no
not you. You were songless,
and in some ways, friendless
as inspiration could not have associated with your image
or handed you a medal, a purple heart, a gold star.
Oh, my dear,
you may be the butt of the joke but
I must say, you are brave.
You stood up for me during those terrible
staff meetings, poised and together deep inside.
When angry teachers bitched and complained,
you quietly lit one and for the time,
kept the room quiet.
Some say if you were stretched from end to end
you would wrap yourself around the earth.
And you are of the earth, a brown hose
of an earthworm, wringing its way inside space

small as a drum. You are the mother of all elimination
nurturing the system as you quietly spit out the toxins.
You are also father snake,
dissolving hate from the gut and dispersing anxiety
which sinks like grit after all the upset.
I guess I must remember all the more
intimate moments of you and me
in the bathrooms of my life and miss you,
or at least, the part of you that was cut away last summer.
For what other organ can do what you do?
You can be chopped smaller and stitched together
like an octopus's arm, and still inch along your day's work.
The lengths you have gone for me,
all of the shits you gave-
I turn to you now in the moment and say,
Thank you, protector of toxins.
Thank you for caring.

The Cult

The cult members looked worried
when they were reminded by a visitor:
Kill your Buddha.

Two Trees

We sit on the patio where the red shirted man
wheels himself out for a smoke.
Look at two trees, gently moving in the wind, two
distinct great ladies with rounded hips
full as summer's end.
Now that you're ninety,
I drink in anything you say-
even your hallucinations are welcome.
I remember the lunches of our lives
Red Lobster, sipping Chardonnay.
I tell you about my life somewhere,
you listen but do not lean in,
lipstick stuck to the glass.
Today those past conversations are shells,
empty of weight, airy
as you breath in the coming fall.
You're down to two eyes looking at two trees
which you say look like sisters.
Leaning in, I saw it too,
saw them as family through your eyes.

I Am Your Bedroom

I am your bedroom, the space that you played in
When you sat on your bed inside, chalk board in your hands
Stuffed animals nearby, you wrote your friends' names
And then their birthdays, practiced your long hand and
Later, math equations.

You were the girl that grew up inside of me
Your body stretched on your four-poster canopy bed
While the brown and white hamsters ran around a little wheel
Squeaking in the night

You were the girl who daydreamed about birth mother
I knew your right side gave you nightmares, you slept in a ball on
     your left
I heard your prayers of thanks to God, and blessings to everyone
     everywhere.
The bear poster you kept for years, yes, Love lasts.

Though I could not imagine a place outside of this home
Or a job more important than raising you into a woman
My purpose was to stand around you, keeping out the thunder
     and the blizzards
The yelling and crying of your mother and father, the slamming
     of the kitchen cabinets.

My job was to bring you some peace as you sat on my navy
    carpet barefooted, practicing the splits, pushing your fingers
    through the plush fabric
You were the teenager who put on makeup with your girlfriends
    and cut each other's hair
Sharing poetry and music, and cigarettes which you'd light out
    the window
The smoke blowing away from me into the night.

I sat alone and empty as you went to college, to London and
    Japan
Sometimes you brought your men to me
You and I mingled, the smells of all of our years together
I remained unchanged with your posters of cats and mountain
    ranges
The Japanese doll standing year after year in the corner,
Psychology books tossed in a box, understood you.

Being your sanctuary for growing, for loving and losing
For everything you learned in me, for everything you realized-
I want to tell you this: I still love you as though you were five
When you didn't know who you were
I knew. I witnessed your truth-
The part that was never in the fog.

Two More Brothers

They pull up the car and collect me
the airport falling back into the night.
My two new brothers are tall.
I cannot fathom this feeling
to be for once on the same level.
Trusted, respected.
Not adopted.
Not different.
Not other.
They are two gifts that have never been opened
with no karma to speak of between us,
no past full of fights.
We look at one another
drink tasty beers in some beautiful space.
I can't stop talking, can't stop taking
in the ease, that summer place.

I have two more brothers.

The world falls away.

A Summer Place

Is it better to have one perfect memory in life
or attempt happiness every day?
Do we strive for happiness because it is our birth right
or because it is the right thing to do?

Is there a summer place that we return to
or just a memory of perfection?

Does anyone have a perfect childhood-
Does anyone fully embody their own body-
Does anyone care for the ancestors?

Does everyone need somewhere to call home-
Does somebody need you to be happy?

Is there a spiritual place around you
or just grasping for perfection?

Can we create joy in this space, here and now?

About the Author

Jill Uchiyama (Skufakiss) was born Susan Thanos in The Bronx in 1968. She grew up in Hammond, Indiana and was educated at Indiana University and Western Michigan University where she received a Master's Degree in Counseling. This is her first book of poetry. In 2018 she discovered her birth family, shortly before turning fifty. This occurred mainly through the help of two cousins who guided her through DNA testing and the understanding of genealogy. This book is dedicated to them and all adoptees and families that have been touched by adoption.

Ms. Uchiyama is also a filmmaker and since 2013 has been commissioned to do Legacy films. Her first film, "The Legacy of Joseph Gifford" was accepted at the New Filmmaker's Film Festival in New York City. Her films have been shared and shown all over the world and are available to watch on Vimeo. She writes grants for Manchester School District in New Hampshire.

Printed in Great Britain
by Amazon

16921592R00043